Compiled, Written and Edited by:
Katie Read
Design and Layout:
Isobel Kinnear
Series Editor: Simon Melhuish

Published by Lagoon Books
UK: PO Box 58528, London SW13 3AY
USA: 10685-B Hazelhurst Dr. #9988
Houston, TX77043

Lagoon Books is a trademark of Lagoon
Trading Company Limited.

Printed in China

ISBN: 978-1-90281-380-6

www.thelagoongroup.com

JOKES
FOR THE JOHN

I'm terrified of **elevators:** I'm taking

....

steps

....

to

avoid them.

Have you heard the conspiracy about *Russian allotments?* It's all just a **communist plot.**

My friends tell me I'm a *skeptic*, but I don't *believe* a word they say.

How did the cat respond to the bad joke? "You have cat to be *KITTEN* me right **MEOW**."

Wanna hear a joke about ghosts? Yes?

That's the spirit!

I ate some ice-cream with a DVD last night. I couldn't be bothered to wash up a . . . .

spoon.
. . . .

If you want to set up a company and run it, that's your own **BUSINESS.**

All those who believe in telekinesis, **raise my hand.**

I saw a film about beavers last weekend. Best

DAM

movie this year.

Why can't you have a nose 12 inches long?

Because then it would be a foot.

I don't understand why people pick their noses ...
I was born with mine.

What

do

you

call

a

frozen

dog?

Pupsicle.

Wind turbines?

BIG FAN.

A man goes to the doctor with a *strawberry* growing on his head. The doctor says, "I'll give you some **cream** to put on it."

Jokes about German sausages are the wurst.

Barman: How would you like to buy a vodka for 20p?
Customer: That's a **CHEAP SHOT** and you know it.

At the scene of the crime, there was what looked like a freshly dug hole. The police are

looking into it...

I looked in your fridge: *soya milk.*

What do you give the man who has everything?

A n t i

b i o t

i c s .

Light travels faster than sound.
That's why some people appear

bright

until you hear them speak.

A termite
walks into
a pub and
asks,
**"is the bar
tender
here?"**

My friend got fired from the circus. He says
he's going to sue them for

FUN-FAIR DISMISSAL.

I heard that Black Beauty is a dark horse.

A clown held open the door for me. I thought it was a

NICE

JESTER.

· · · · · ·

Knowledge is understanding that a tomato is a fruit. Wisdom is not putting it in a fruit salad.

What's the difference between a well-dressed man, and a well-dressed man on a unicycle?

ATTIRE!

Need an ark? I Noah guy

!

What should you do with dead chemists?
Barium.

A man ended up in hospital today covered in wood and hay, and with a horse inside him. His condition is described as

stable.

What does a house wear?

ADDRESS.

Which knight built King Arthur's round table?

Sir Cumference.

I bought a dog from an ironmonger the other day. As soon as I got him home,

he made a bolt for the door.

Making lasagne by myself always makes me feel *cannelloni.*

Farmer Giles: I can't decide whether to buy a bicycle or a cow for the farm.

Farmer Miles: You'd look silly riding a cow.

Farmer Giles: I'd look even sillier milking a bicycle.

IF BARBIE IS SO POPULAR, WHY DO I HAVE TO BUY HER FRIENDS?

I watched Jurassic park yesterday. Not only does he have a weird name, but ～ he's a ～ **terrible driver too.**

What did the starfish say to the sea cucumber?

KEEP YOUR FRONDS CLOSE AND YOUR ANEMONES CLOSER.

If you don't know what to buy someone for Christmas, just get them a fridge and watch their **face light up when they open it.**

Why don't owls like dating in the rain?

Because it's too wet to woo.

I can't stand Russian dolls. They're so full of themselves.

Why did the banana go to the doctor? He wasn't *peeling well.*

I TRIED TO HIDE MY SOAP ADDICTION FROM MY FAMILY. BUT I'VE DECIDED TO COME CLEAN.

Son: There's a man at the door collecting for the old folks' home.

Dad:

Give him Granny.

Pink Panther's to do list:
◇◇◇ to do, ◇◇◇
to do,
to do, to do, to do,
to do, to dooooo!

Santa's little helpers?

You mean subordinate clauses?

What bird is always out of breath?

A puffin.

It was really hard getting over my addiction to the hokey-kokey,

but I turned myself around and that's what it's all about.

Whoever stole my copy of Microsoft Office is in big trouble.

YOU HAVE MY WORD.

A magician was driving down the road, then he turned into a driveway.

This girl said she recognized me from the *vegetarian* club. I didn't think I'd met **herbivore.**

What kind of tea is hard to swallow? **REALITY.**

I BOUGHT SOME SHOES FROM A DRUG DEALER. I DON'T KNOW WHAT HE LACED THEM WITH BUT I'VE BEEN TRIPPING ALL DAY.

Want to hear a toilet joke?

URINE LUCK.

Why does Snoop Dogg carry an umbrella? **Fo' drizzle.**

There are three types of people in this world. **Those who can count, and those who can't.**

BECOMING A VEGETARIAN IS A HUGE

MISSED STEAK.

What's the difference between roast beef and pea soup?
Anyone can roast beef.

Here's a bit of advice for you.

Advi-

What did the duck say to the bartender?

◇◇◇◇◇◇◇◇◇◇◇◇◇◇◇

Put it on my bill.

◇◇◇◇◇◇◇◇◇◇◇◇◇◇◇

How do trees feel in the spring?
Re-leaved.

Did you hear about the dyslexic, agnostic, insomniac?
He lies awake at night wondering whether there's a dog.

People call me
Mr. Compromise.
It wasn't my first choice of nickname,
but I can live with it.

● ● ● ● ● ● ● ● ● ●

When's the best
time to go to the
~ dentist? ~

TWO -THIRTY.

What's
orange
and
sounds
like a
parrot?
A carrot.

Time flies like an arrow.
Fruit flies like a banana.

Iron Man and the Silver Surfer have teamed up.

THEY'RE
ALLOYS!

I made a chicken salad on Friday.
He still hasn't thanked me.

Which farmer sits on his tractor shouting,

"THE END IS NIGH!"?

Farmer Geddon.

If you have to borrow money, borrow from a pessimist. They wont expect it back.

I'm reading this book about anti-gravity. It's impossible ~ to ~ **put down.**

A man sitting in a bar keeps hearing a voice telling him how handsome he is. **"Who's saying that?"** he asks the barman. **"It's the peanuts, sir. They're complimentary!"**

So, if you could just rehydrate those raisins, that would be

GRAPES.

To neigh, or not to neigh: that is equestrian.

A BOILED EGG IN THE MORNING IS HARD TO BEAT.

A dolphin swims up to 3 orcas and says,

"Whale, whale, whale. What have we got here?"

What did the ocean say to the beach? **Nothing, it just waved.**

- - - - -

A ground-breaking invention?

- - - - -

THE

SHOVEL.

How should you approach an angry Welsh cheese?

Caerphilly.

I JUST SWAPPED OUR BED FOR A TRAMPOLINE. MY BOYFRIEND HIT THE ROOF.

Atheism is a non-prophet organization.

Beaver: Wanna help me gnaw down this tree?

Otter: I think you've confused me with someone who builds a dam.

⬦⬦⬦

Went to a corner shop - bought 4 corners.

I gave away
all my dead
batteries
today.

FREE OF
CHARGE.

*If you think
you can
survive on
just water,
you're
diluting
yourself.*

I'd like to die like
my grandfather;
peacefully in his
~~ sleep. ~~

***Not screaming
like his
passengers.***

My boyfriend said we would have less arguments if wasn't so pedantic. I said,

"Fewer arguments."

Shakespeare walks into a pub. The landlord points at him and shouts

Ya bard!

Why did the paranoid man leave Twitter?

He thought he was being followed.

Cremation.
Thinking outside of the box.

I often
eat
seafood
just
for the
halibut.
• • • • • • •

I decided to get rid of my vacuum cleaner.
It was just collecting dust.

Melon 1:

Let's run away and get married!

Melon 2:

I'm sorry but I

Cantaloupe.

DID YOU
HEAR ABOUT
THE FIRE AT
THE CIRCUS.

THE HEAT
WAS IN
TENTS.

Pancake day.
That creped up on us...

What did the chicken say about the **scrambled egg?**

There goes my crazy mixed up kid.

What lies at the bottom of the ocean and twitches?

A nervous wreck.

What did the pirate say on his 80th birthday?

Aye matey!

What's green and stands in the corner?

A naughty frog.

It was an emotional wedding. **Even the cake was in tiers.**

I'D KILL FOR A NOBEL PEACE PRIZE .

Koala: What do you mean I'm not a bear? I have all the koalafications!

Elephant: You're koalafications are totally irrelephant.

Bear: Stop arguing! It's unbearable!

Otter: I agree, you otter be ashamed of yourselves. I'm leaving.

Alpaca: Alpaca your things.

HAVING SEX IN AN ELEVATOR IS WRONG ON SO MANY LEVELS.

A book fell on my head yesterday. *I guess I only have my shelf to blame.*

HAVE YOU HEARD OF THE
MOVIE 'CONSTIPATION'?

THAT'S BECAUSE
IT HASN'T COME
OUT YET.

*My therapist says I have a
preoccupation with vengeance.
We'll see about that...*

What's a cannibal's favorite
party game?

SWALLOW
~THE~
LEADER.

Why do Marxists hate loose-leaf tea?

BECAUSE PROPER TEA IS THEFT.

||||||||||||||||||
Why are there so many different types of pasta?

If I had *a penne* for every time I've asked myself that question…
||||||||||||||||||||

My friend dug a hole in the garden and filled it with water.

~~~ ~~~

I think she meant well.

I asked for something Cuban for Christmas, and my mum bought me a Che Guevara t-shirt. Clothes, but no cigar.

I wondered why the frisbee was getting **bigger,** *then it hit me.*

BAKERS TRADE RECIPES ON A KNEAD TO KNOW BASIS.

4 out of 5 people will suffer from warts at some point in their life. 1 in 5 people will really enjoy them.

The Queen wakes up, looks out of the window, and says,

LOOK
LIKE
ANOTHER
REIGNY
DAY

The worst thing about throwing a party in space?

YOU HAVE TO PLANET.

"Hi, you're through to the incontinence hotline. Can you hold please?"

My friend bought himself a cardboard belt.

What a waist of paper!

What's the difference between *a guitar and a fish?*

You can't tuna fish.

Sign language? Very handy.

MY SEASICKNESS COMES IN WAVES.

What do you call a posh Gym?
James.

Did you hear about the scarecrow who won an award?

IT WAS FOR BEING OUTSTANDING IN HIS FIELD.

What's brown and sounds like a bell?

Dung.

CAN FEBRUARY MARCH?
NO, BUT APRIL MAY.

WHITEBOARDS ARE REMARKABLE.

Dad: *Hey, look! There's a flock of cows!*
Son: *Herd of cows, dad.*
Dad: *Heard of them? There's a whole flock right there!*

THE UNIVERSE IMPLODES: NO MATTER.

I've always thought that manufacturing tabletops is **counterproductive.**

~~~ • • • ~~~

◇◇◇◇◇◇◇◇

My dog,
Minton,
ate a
racket.
**Bad
Minton.**

◇◇◇◇◇◇◇◇

Pediatricians are doctors with little patience.

I submitted ten puns to a local newspaper that was giving away $100 for the best joke. Despite multiple efforts to win,

no pun in ten did.

How many tickles does it take to make an octopus laugh?

Tentacles.

A skeleton walks into a pub and asks for a pint of lager and a mop.

Two fish are in a tank. One says to the other,

· · · · · · · · ·

"Uhm, do you know how to drive this thing?"

· · · · · · · · ·

It's hard to explain jokes to a *kleptomaniac.* They always take ~ things ~ ***literally.***

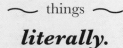

I DONUT UNDERSTAND FOOD PUNS.

Did you hear about
the fight between
the dentist
and
the manicurist.

**They fought
tooth and
nail.**

What's Beethoven's
favorite fruit?
Ba-na-na-na!

*My brother caught me rummaging around in
his wardrobe the other day. He asked me what
I was doing, I said,*

"It's Narnia business."

POOR OLD DARTH VADER; LOOKING FOR LOVE IN ALDERAAN PLACES.

What do you call a tiny collection of galaxies.
The puny-verse.

Which breed of
dog makes the best
magician?

〜〜〜 ◇◇◇ 〜〜〜

**The
Labracadabrador.**

What do you call a broken can-opener?

A can't-opener.

Two hydrogen atoms walk into a bar.
One says,
"I think I've lost an electron."
The others says,
"Are you sure?"
"Yes,"
replies the first atom,
"I'm positive."

Mum asked me to put the kettle on, but it didn't fit.

SOMEBODY ATTACKED ME IN THE PARK WITH A BAT. TO BE FAIR, I WAS QUITE IMPRESSED BY HOW WELL HE'D TRAINED IT.

Did you hear about the child who refused to take a nap? *He was charged with resisting a rest.*

Why did the doll blush?
~~~ She saw the ~~~
teddy bare.

Two whales walk into a bar. The first whale says *"OOOOEEEEE AAAAYYYY UUUUUAAAA EEEEOOO!"* The second whale says, *"Shut up, Steve, you're drunk."*

My friend and I were fighting over which is the best vowel. I won.

I can't work out why someone keeps adding soil to my allotment. ***The plot thickens…***

What do you call a *retired vegetable?*

— ∞ —

A has-bean.

I've accidentally swallowed some Scrabble tiles.
My next crap could spell disaster.

When my girlfriend said she was leaving me because of my obsession with The Monkees I thought she was joking.

And then I saw her face.

Studies show that six out of seven dwarves aren't Happy.

I'VE LOST MY MOOD RING. I'M REALLY NOT SURE HOW I FEEL ABOUT IT.

◇◇◇◇◇◇◇◇◇◇◇◇◇

Johnny:

Sir, can I go to the bathroom?

Teacher:

Johnny, MAY I go to the bathroom!?

Johnny:

But Sir, I asked first!

◇◇◇◇◇◇◇◇◇◇◇◇◇

PRETENTIOUS? MOI?

My new stereo system came with a broken volume dial, but only cost me a dollar.

~ • • • ~

For that price, I couldn't turn it down.

What do you call the dangerous Italian area of town?

The Spaghetto.

I went to buy a Christmas tree, and the guy asked me *"are you going to put it up yourself?"* ∼ I said, ∼ **"don't be disgusting, I'm putting it in the living room."**

I have **kleptomania.** When it gets really ◇◇◇◇◇ bad, ◇◇◇◇◇ *I take something for it.*

WHAT'S THE MOST COMMONLY MISSPELLED BLOOD GROUP?

TYPO.

The early
bird may
get the
worm, but
the second
mouse gets
the cheese.

Did you hear about the
big paddle sale?
It was quite an oardeal.

Why did the mushroom go
to the party?
Because he was a fungi.
Why did he leave?
There wasn't mushroom.

Why couldn't the lifeguard save the hippie?

He was too far out, *man.*

I took the shell off my snail to make him go faster, but he's ***even more sluggish than before.***

"You wont like me when I'm angry. My rage is always well founded, and backed up with reliable sources," said **the Credible Hulk.**

Always make sure to tip your exorcist, so that you don't get repossessed.

Captain Hook walks into a pizza restaurant.
Waiter:
What can I get you today?
Captain Hook:
I'd like a large Pepperoni pizza.
Waiter:
No problem, would you like that to be deep dish or pan?
Captain Hook:
GIVE ME PAN!!!!!

PAVLOV? YEAH, RINGS A BELL...

Did you hear about
the dyslexic devil-worshipper?
He sold his soul to Santa.

So what if I can't spell 'Armageddon'?
It's not the end of the world...

I'd like to get into
juggling, but I've

never
had the
balls
for it.

The other day, someone left some modeling clay at my house. ～～ **I didn't know what to make of it.**

◇◇◇

What's *square* and *green*?
A lemon in disguise.

This Christmas I'm going to put up a marquee in my garden with some funky music, dry ice and laser lights. Now is the winter of my disco tent.

First rule of Thesaurus Club:

You don't talk, converse, discuss, speak, chat, deliberate, confer, gab, gossip or natter about Thesaurus Club.

Bladder infection?
Oh, urine trouble.

I can't stand street performers.

Then again,

I'm a mime, so I can't really talk.

I got hit with some Omega 3 pills this morning. Luckily, I only suffered

SUPER FISH OIL INJURIES.

Why was the archaeologist depressed?
Her career was in ruins.

Did you hear about the cannibal who was late for dinner?

He got the cold shoulder.

I play the triangle for a reggae band. It's pretty relaxed:

I just stand at the back and
TING.

What did one toilet say to the other?

"YOU LOOK FLUSHED."

Sleeping comes naturally to me.
I can do it with my eyes closed.

They've discovered a new disease living in margarine. Apparently it's **spreading very quickly.**

Somebody called me pretentious the other day. I nearly choked on my decaf soya latte.

"Do you want to come to my yoga class with me?"

"Namaste here."

I can't face making any
more donuts.

**I'm tired of the
hole thing.**

What's the difference between
pizza and pizza jokes?
Pizza jokes can't be topped.

Nostalgia isn't what it used to be...

Toilet paper:

what a rip-off.

How do you threaten a calendar?
Tell him his days are numbered.

What do you get if
you walk under a
cow?

~ • • • ~

**A pat on the
head.**

*Sometimes
I squat on the floor,
wrap my arms
around my legs and
lean forwards.*

**That's how
I roll.**

Best thing
about living in
Switzerland?
Well, the flag
is a

big plus.

How do you make antifreeze?

STEAL HER BLANKET.

SHE WAS ONLY A WHISKEY MAKER, BUT HE LOVED HER STILL.

A shop assistant dared to ask me why I was buying 20 pots of Tipp-Ex.

Big mistake.

The past, present and future walked into a bar.
It was tense.

"I HATE TACOS"...
SAID NO JUAN EVER.

Two vultures board an airplane, each carrying two dead raccoons. The stewardess looks at them and says,
"I'm sorry, gentlemen, only one carrion allowed per passenger."

What do you get if you cross a joke with a rhetorical question?

Sure, I could make a pencil with rubbers at both ends, but what would be the point?

MY LIMBO TEAM AND I GO WAY BACK.

A Buddhist walks into a pizza restaurant, and says,

• • •

"make me one with everything."

I remember the first time I saw a universal remote. I thought,

"Wow, this changes everything."

I had some mushrooms this morning:

BREAKFAST OF CHAMPIGNONS

How does Good King Wenceslas like his pizza?

DEEP PAN, CRISP AND EVEN.

Did you hear about those new corduroy pillowcases?

They're making headlines.

Daughter: *Can we have a dog for Christmas?*
Mother: *No, darling, we'll have a turkey like everyone else.*

My computer beat me at chess, so I challenged it to a boxing match.

· ·

CONSTIPATION: SAME SHIT. DIFFERENT DAY.

A G N B.

That's bang out of order.

I could never work out how to use a seatbelt, then one day it **clicked.**

I quit my job at the helium factory.
I wasn't going to be spoken to in that tone.

A woman complaining to her husband says, "Look at Mr. Barnes across the road. Every morning when he goes to work he kisses his wife goodbye. Why don't you ever do that?" "Because," her husband says,

"I haven't been introduced to her yet."

◇◇◇

A random email address keeps sending me pictures of canned meat.

I hate spam.

What's red and invisible?

• •

NO TOMATOES.

Waiter! This coffee tastes like mud.
Yes sir, it's fresh ground.

◇◇◇◇◇◇◇◇◇◇◇◇◇◇◇◇◇◇◇◇◇◇◇◇◇◇◇◇◇◇◇◇◇◇◇◇

What's yellow, hot, and
highly dangerous?

~ • • • ~

**Shark-infested
custard.**

Have you heard about the magic tractor? **It turned into a field.**

What did the cheese say to a bear that was stuck in a tree?

"Camembert!"

What's red and bad for your teeth?

Bricks.

A couple of cows are talking in the field. One says,
"Have you heard about that mad cow disease going around?"
The other cow says,
"Yeah. Makes me glad I'm a penguin."

Where can you find a dog with no legs?
Right where you left him.

How many ears does Mr. Spock have?
Three.
A left ear, a right ear, and a final front ear.

What do you get if you pour boiling water down a rabbits' hole?

HOT CROSS BUNNIES.

Waiter! There's a fly in my soup!
Not, so loud, sir, or they'll all want one.

Two rabbits were chased by a pack of wolves into a forest. One rabbit turned to the other and said,

"Shall we make a run for it, or stay here for a few days and outnumber them?"

Why do gorillas
have big nostrils?
Because they
have big fingers.

I was on my way to
work the other day,
when this kid threw a
piece of cheddar at me!

*I didn't think it
was very mature.*

What did the cheese say when he
saw himself in the mirror?

"HALLOUMI!"

Waiter, is there soup on the menu?

No madam, I wiped it off.

A bear walks into a bar and says,
*"I'd like a beer.......... and some
of those peanuts."*
The bartender says,
***"Sure, but why the
big paws?"***

Why shouldn't you date
a tennis player?
*Because love means
nothing to them.*

What kind of cheese
conceals horses?

MASCARPONE.

*A priest, a rabbi, and an
imam walk into a bar. The
barmaid says,*
**"Is this some sort
of joke?"**

Why did the turkey cross
the road?
**To prove he wasn't
chicken.**

The nurse next door has changed her name to *'Appendix'*.

~~~ ◊◊◊ ~~~

She's hoping a surgeon will take her out.

What's brown and runs around the garden?

A fence.

A man goes to the doctor's with a cucumber up his nose, a carrot in his left ear and a banana in his right ear. *"What's the matter with me?"* he asks. The doctor replies, **"You're not eating properly."**

What's the difference between a well-dressed man, and a tired dog?

ONE WEARS A SUIT; THE OTHER JUST PANTS.

Where does a general keep his armies?

~ ◇ ~

Up his sleevies!

A sandwich walks into a bar and the landlord says, *"Sorry, we don't serve food."*

How many psychiatrists does it take to change a light bulb?

Only one, but it has to really want to change.

What did the hat say to the scarf?

◇◇◇

"You hang around, I'll go on ahead."

Why do cows wear bells?

Because their horns don't work.

Why are jumpers
bad at Articulate?

**Because
they're
knit-wits.**

*A dyslexic
man
walks
into a bra.*

*How many surrealists does it take to screw
in a lightbulb?*
**Two: One to comfort the fish,
the other to put the giraffes in
the bath.**

A German walks into a bar and asks for a martini.
The bartender asks,
"Dry?"
He replies,
"Nein, just one."

When I heard that Oxygen and Magnesium were getting together, I was like

OMg.

I don't trust graphs…
They're always plotting something.

What do you call a
man with no shins?

TONY.

WHAT DO
YOU CALL
POSTMAN
PAT ON
HIS DAY
OFF?

PAT.

Did you know I have a step-ladder?
Yeah, it's a shame I never knew
my real ladder.

Four fonts walk into
a bar, the barman
~~ says ~~
**"Get out!
We don't want your
type in here."**

● ● ●

I'm trying to pack myself in a
small suitcase.
I can hardly contain myself.

— — — — — — — — — —

*A lorry-load of tortoises crashed into
a trainload of terrapins.*

IT WAS A TURTLE DISASTER.

What do killer whales look for most when house hunting?

SEALINGS.

Two cannibals are eating a clown. One turns to the other and says,

"Does this taste funny to you?"

WHAT DID THE CLIFF-HANGER SAY TO THE CROWD?

Pavlov is sitting in a bar, enjoying a pint when the phone rings. He jumps up shouting, **"I forgot to feed the dog!"**

What's green and has wheels? **Grass. *I lied about the wheels.***

What's the difference between arrogance and apathy?

I don't know, and I don't care.

A pun, a play on words, and a limerick walk into a bar. *No joke.*

I've got a friend who's fallen in love with two school bags,

he's bisatchel.

I WAS GOING TO BUY A POCKET CALCULATOR. BUT THEN I THOUGHT. WHO CARES HOW MANY POCKETS I HAVE?

People often accuse me of "stealing others jokes" and being a "plagiarist".

Their words not mine...

• • • • • • • • • • • • • •

I'm on a whiskey diet. I've lost three days already.

I said to ticket sales
"I want to go to Paris".
He said "Eurostar?"
I said,
"Well, I've been on TV."